my **revision** notes

Edexcel GCSE (9–1) History

SUPERPOWER RELATIONS AND THE COLD WAR
1941–91

Steve Waugh

HODDER
EDUCATION
AN HACHETTE UK COMPANY

The Publishers would like to thank the following for permission to reproduce copyright material.

Acknowledgements: mark schemes reproduced by kind permission of Pearson Education Ltd

Every effort has been made to trace all copyright holders, but if any have been inadvertently overlooked, the Publishers will be pleased to make the necessary arrangements at the first opportunity.

Although every effort has been made to ensure that website addresses are correct at time of going to press, Hodder Education cannot be held responsible for the content of any website mentioned in this book. It is sometimes possible to find a relocated web page by typing in the address of the home page for a website in the URL window of your browser.

Hachette UK's policy is to use papers that are natural, renewable and recyclable products and made from wood grown in sustainable forests. The logging and manufacturing processes are expected to conform to the environmental regulations of the country of origin.

Orders: please contact Bookpoint Ltd, 130 Milton Park, Abingdon, Oxon OX14 4SE. Telephone: +44 (0)1235 827720. Fax: +44 (0)1235 400454. Email education@bookpoint.co.uk Lines are open from 9 a.m. to 5 p.m., Monday to Saturday, with a 24-hour message answering service. You can also order through our website: www.hoddereducation.co.uk

ISBN: 978 1 5104 0325 3

© Steve Waugh

First published in 2017 by
Hodder Education
An Hachette UK Company
Carmelite House, 50 Victoria Embankment
London EC4Y 0DZ

www.hoddereducation.co.uk

Impression number   10 9 8 7 6 5 4 3
Year   2021 2020 2019 2018

Cover photo © J. Helgason/Shutterstock
Illustrations by Gray Publishing
Produced and typeset in Bembo by Gray Publishing, Tunbridge Wells, Kent
Printed in Spain

A catalogue record for this title is available from the British Library.

How to get the most out of this book

This book will help you revise for the modern depth study Superpower relations and the Cold War, 1941–91.

Use the revision planner on pages 2–3 to track your progress, topic by topic. Tick each box when you have:

1 revised and understood each topic

2 completed the activities

3 checked your answers online.

The content in the book is organised into a series of double-page spreads which cover the content in the specification. The left-hand page on each spread has the key content for each topic, and the right-hand page has one or two activities to help you with exam skills or to learn the knowledge you need. Answers to these activities can be found on pages 39–47. Quick multiple-choice quizzes to test your knowledge of each topic can be found on the website.

At the end of the book is an exam focus section (pages 32–38) which gives you guidance on how to answer each exam question type.

There are a variety of **activities** for you to complete related to the content on the left-hand page. Some are based on **exam-style questions** which aim to consolidate your revision and practise your exam skills. Others are **revision tasks** to make sure that you have understood every topic and to help you record the key information about each topic.

Tick to track your progress as you revise each element of the key content.

Content for each topic is on the left-hand page.

Key terms and **Key individuals** are highlighted in the section colour the first time they appear, with an explanation nearby in the margin. As you work through this book, highlight other key ideas and add your own notes. Make this *your* book.

Shorter **revision tasks** help you remember key points of content.

Throughout the book there are **exam tips** that remind you of key points that will help you in the exam.

Contents and revision planner

REVISED

Quick quizzes at **www.hoddereducation.co.uk/myrevisionnotes**

Key topic 3: The end of the Cold War, 1970–91

Exam focus

Question 1: Consequence
Question 2: Narrative account
Question 3: Importance

Revision techniques

Answers

Key topic 1 The origins of the Cold War, 1941–58

The **Cold War** began in 1945–46 following the Second World War. Ideological differences between the **superpowers** led to clashes over Berlin and the formation of rival military blocs. The Cold War intensified with the Soviet invasion of Hungary in 1956.

1 Early tension between East and West 1

REVISED

1.1 The ideological differences between the superpowers

Ideological differences caused mistrust between the superpowers, and meant they had different aims about post-war Europe. The USA feared the spread of communism; the Soviet Union wanted communist satellite states to prevent future invasions.

	Communism (Soviet Union)	Capitalism (USA)
Politics	Only one political party – the Communist Party	Several parties – voters choose and change their governments
Economy	All industry and businesses owned by the state for the benefit of everyone Everyone equal	Most industry and businesses privately owned Some will be wealthier than others
Influence	Encourage communism in other countries	Encourage trade with other countries

1.2 The Grand Alliance

The leaders of the **Grand Alliance** met in three conferences, where differences emerged.

The Tehran Conference, 1943

The first meeting of the Big Three – Stalin (leader of the Soviet Union), Roosevelt (US president) and Churchill (British prime minister). It was agreed:

- A second front would be opened in France in May 1944.
- The Soviet Union would enter the war against Japan after Germany's defeat.
- A **United Nations Organisation** would be set up after the war.
- Poland's post-war borders would be along the Oder and Neisse rivers; adding an area of eastern Poland to the Soviet Union.

The Yalta Conference, February 1945

Agreements at the conference	Disagreements at the conference
The Declaration of Liberated Europe – to aid all peoples liberated from Nazi control	Stalin wanted a higher figure of German **reparations** than Roosevelt or Churchill
The Soviet Union would enter the war against Japan after Germany's defeat	
To divide Germany and Berlin into four zones	Stalin wanted the Polish border to be further west and a 'friendly' Polish government. But he agreed to free elections
To hunt down and try Nazi war criminals	
To allow free elections in countries liberated from German occupation	
Setting up a United Nations Organisation	

Key terms

Cold War War waged against an enemy by every means short of fighting each other. Used to describe the relationship between the USA and Soviet Union 1945–91

Grand Alliance Alliance of the Soviet Union, USA and Britain during the Second World War

Reparations Compensation to be paid to other countries by Germany after the Second World War

Superpower A country or state that has great global power – in 1945, the USA and Soviet Union

United Nations Organisation International body set up in 1945 to promote peace and international cooperation and security

The attitudes of Stalin, Truman and Churchill

- Roosevelt died in April 1945 and the new president, Truman, distrusted Stalin. He was convinced that the Soviet Union intended to take over Europe and he was determined to stand up to Stalin.

- Stalin suspected that the West did not want a strong Soviet Union. He wanted Soviet-controlled communist governments in Eastern Europe as a defence against future attacks. Before the Potsdam Conference the USA had successfully tested the atomic bomb. Stalin was furious that Truman hadn't consulted him. He thought that the USA was using the bomb as a warning.

- Churchill was suspicious of Stalin's motives. He thought that Soviet troops would remain in the Eastern European countries they had liberated from the Germans.

Clement Attlee replaced Churchill as British prime minister during the Potsdam Conference.

Exam tip

Students often confuse the key features of the Yalta and Potsdam conferences. Ensure you know who attended and what was agreed at each.

The Potsdam Conference, July 1945

Agreements at the conference	Disagreements at the conference
To divide Germany and Berlin into four zones	Stalin wanted massive compensation from Germany. Truman refused, seeing a revived Germany as a possible barrier to future Soviet expansion
Germany to pay reparations in equipment and materials	
De-Nazification: Nazi Party banned; Nazis removed from important positions; leading Nazis put on trial for war crimes	
To move Poland's border west – along the Oder and Neisse rivers	Truman wanted free elections in Eastern European countries occupied by Soviet troops. Stalin did not
Full participation in the United Nations Organisation	

Memory map

Create a memory map to show the main ideological differences between the USA and the Soviet Union. Add some key words from the information on page 4 and your own knowledge to a copy of the diagram in this box. Highlight which differences you think were most important in causing the Cold War.

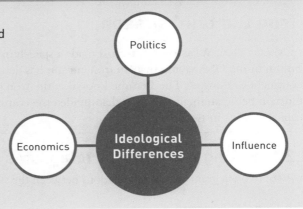

Politics

Economics

Ideological Differences

Influence

Organising knowledge

Using the information on pages 4 and 5, copy and complete the table below to summarise the key features of the conferences held between the Grand Alliance during and after the Second World War and to make a judgement on how important they were in causing tensions between the superpowers.

	Tehran	Yalta	Potsdam
Points agreed			
Areas of disagreement			
Importance in causing tensions			

2 Early tension between East and West 2

2.1 The creation of Soviet satellite states

In the years immediately following the end of the Second World War, the Soviet Union expanded its influence in Eastern Europe. This expansion was due to the Soviet desire for security. The Soviet Union had been invaded by Germany on two occasions – 1914 and 1941 – and had suffered huge casualties in the ensuing world wars. **Stalin** created Soviet-controlled states in Eastern Europe as a buffer against future invasions.

● Elections were held in each Eastern European country but were rigged to ensure that Soviet-controlled Communist parties took over.

● By 1948, Soviet **satellite states** with communist governments were established across Eastern Europe (see box).

Soviet satellite states

Albania, Bulgaria, Czechoslovakia, East Germany (from 1949 the German Democratic Republic), Hungary, Poland, Romania.

Consequences

● Security for the Soviet Union. Eastern Europe could now act as a buffer against a possible future invasion from the West.

● Increased rivalry. The USA, Britain and France believed that Stalin's motives were political – the expansion of the Soviet empire and communism throughout Europe, as shown in Long telegram.

● The Soviet Union now had control of Eastern Europe. This confirmed the divisions between East and West stated in Churchill's 'Iron Curtain' speech.

'Iron Curtain' speech

In March 1946, **Winston Churchill** made a speech in the small town of Fulton in the USA saying that 'an iron curtain has descended across the continent of Europe'. This became known as the Iron Curtain speech, the Iron Curtain being an imaginary line that divided the communist East from the capitalist West in Europe.

2.2 The Long and Novikov telegrams

In 1946, two telegrams worsened relations between the superpowers.

The Long telegram

George Kennan was the USA's Deputy Chief of Mission at the US embassy in Moscow. He saw the Soviet Union as aggressive and suspicious and recommended firm action against Soviet expansion in Eastern Europe. His telegram, which became known as the Long telegram, greatly influenced **Truman**'s policies in the Cold War, especially his policy of **containment**.

Novikov telegram

The Soviet Union knew about the Long Telegram. It retaliated with the Novikov telegram. This was written by Nikolai Novikov, the Soviet ambassador to the USA. He accused the USA of trying to achieve world dominance.

Key terms

Containment US policy to use its influence and military resources to prevent the spread of communism into non-communist countries

Satellite state A country under the influence or control of another state

Revision task

1 Using pages 4 and 6, create a timeline showing the key developments in relations between the superpowers in the years 1943–46.

2 Make a list of the consequences of the creation of Soviet-controlled satellite states in Eastern Europe.

Key individuals

Winston Churchill An experienced British politician who was appointed prime minister in 1940, and replaced by Clement Atlee in 1945. He was strongly opposed to communism

Joseph Stalin Succeeded Lenin as leader of the Soviet Union. He served as leader until his death in 1953. He was determined to prevent another invasion of the Soviet Union from the West

Harry S. Truman US president, April 1945 to January 1953. He was strongly opposed to the spread of communism

Eliminate irrelevance

1 Below are an exam-style question and part of an answer. Some parts of the answer aren't relevant to the question. Identify these and draw a line through the information that is irrelevant, justifying your deletions in the margin.

Explain two consequences of the creation of Soviet-controlled satellite states in Eastern Europe.

> The Soviet Union took control of the countries in Eastern Europe by rigging elections to ensure that Soviet-controlled Communist parties took over. These countries included Bulgaria, Romania, Hungary, Poland and Czechoslovakia.
>
> One of the consequences of the creation of these states was security for the Soviet Union. The Soviet Union had been invaded from the west by Germany on two occasions, in 1914 and 1941, and had suffered huge casualties during the ensuing world wars. Stalin created Soviet-controlled states in Eastern Europe as a buffer against future invasions.
>
> The Novikov telegram was written by Nikolai Novikov, who was the Soviet ambassador to the USA at the time. He accused the USA of trying to achieve world dominance. Another consequence was increased rivalry. The USA, Britain and France believed that Stalin's motives were political – the expansion of the Soviet empire and communism throughout Europe.

2 Now have a go at the following question by using the writing frame below.

Explain two consequences of the Potsdam Conference.

What is the first consequence I will explain?

_____

Details to support this consequence:

_____

What is the second consequence I will explain?

_____

Details to support this consequence:

_____

In the balance

1 Using the information on pages 4 and 6, copy and complete both sides of the scales to show who was most to blame for the early Cold War.

2 Overall, who was most to blame for the early Cold War? Explain your judgement.

actions taken by the USA

actions taken by the Soviet Union

3 The development of the Cold War 1

The rivalry between the superpowers intensified in the years 1947–49.

3.1 The Truman Doctrine, 1947

In 1947, Truman began a US policy of containment:

- This was because the USA, and especially Truman, believed that the Soviet Union was trying to spread communism, and also because Greece was being threatened with a communist takeover. By early 1947, Britain told the USA that it could no longer afford to support the Greek and Turkish governments.
- Truman announced US support for Greece in an important speech in March 1947 which became known as the **Truman Doctrine**.

The consequences of the Truman Doctrine

- The Greek government was able to defeat the communists.
- The rivalry between the USA and the Soviet Union increased and the doctrine confirmed the division of the world into communist and non-communist.
- The USA became committed to the policy of containment and far more involved in European affairs.
- The USA decided on the Marshall Plan and Stalin set up **Cominform**.

3.2 The Marshall Plan, 1947

Truman backed up his policy of containment with economic aid to Europe. This was known as the Marshall Plan.

Why was the Marshall Plan introduced?

- Truman believed that communism generally won support in countries where there were economic problems, unemployment and poverty. Many European countries had suffered badly as a result of the Second World War and were struggling to deal with the damage caused.
- If the USA could help these countries to recover economically and provide employment and reasonable prosperity, then there would be no need to turn to communism.

Consequences of the Marshall Plan

- By 1953, the USA had provided $17 billion of aid to rebuild economies and raise standards of living.
- Europe became more firmly divided between East and West. Stalin prevented Eastern European countries, such as Czechoslovakia and Poland, from becoming involved.
- Stalin accused the USA of using the plan for its own selfish interests – to dominate Europe and boost the US economy.

3.3 Cominform and Comecon

The Soviet Union retaliated by setting up rival organisations.

Cominform	Comecon
Cominform was the Communist Information Bureau and was set up in 1947 to enable the Soviet Union to co-ordinate Communist parties throughout Europe. It was the Soviet Union's response to the Truman Doctrine. It was introduced to ensure that the states in Eastern Europe followed Soviet aims in foreign policy	Comecon was the Soviet response to the Marshall Plan. The Council for Mutual Assistance (Comecon) was founded in 1949. It was supposed to be a means by which the Soviet Union could financially support countries in Eastern Europe. In reality, it was used by the Soviet Union to control the economies of these states

Key terms

Comecon The Council for Mutual Assistance

Cominform The Communist Information Bureau

Truman Doctrine US President Truman's idea that it was the USA's duty to prevent the spread of communism to Eastern Europe and the rest of the world. To do this, he was prepared to engage the USA in military enterprises all over the world

Revision task

The Truman Doctrine and Marshall Plan were described as two sides of one coin. Sketch your own coin big enough to write on. On one side give a brief definition of the Truman Doctrine. On the other side give a brief definition of the Marshall Plan.

Exam tip

Students often confuse the Truman Doctrine and the Marshall Plan. Ensure you have a thorough knowledge of both. Remember that the Truman Doctrine is political aid to Western Europe to stop the spread of communism and the Marshall Plan is economic aid.

RAG: Rate the timeline

Below are an exam-style question and a timeline. Read the question, study the timeline and, using three coloured pens, put a **red**, **amber** or **green** star next to the events to show:

Red: events and policies that have **no** relevance to the question

Amber: events and policies that have **some** relevance to the question

Green: events and policies that have **direct** relevance to the question

Write a narrative account analysing the key ways in which the Cold War developed in the years 1945–47.

> You may use the following information in your answer.
> - The Potsdam Conference   ■ The Marshall Plan
> You **must** also use information of your own.

1945 The Yalta Conference

1945 The USA exploded the first atomic bombs

1947 Truman Doctrine and Marshall Plan

1941 The formation of the Grand Alliance

1943 The Tehran Conference

1945 The Potsdam Conference

1947 The setting up of Cominform

1949 The setting up of NATO

1955 The setting up of the Warsaw Pact

1941	1942	1943	1944	1945	1946	1947	1948	1949	1950	1951	1952	1953	1954	1955	1956

1946 Long and Novikov telegrams

1948 Beginning of Berlin blockade

1956 The Hungarian uprising

Adding a third factor

To answer the narrative account style question, you need to explain three developments. It is sensible to make use of the two given points. However, you need to explain a third development. In the space below, write down your choice for a third development in answer to the exam-style question in the 'Rate the timeline' activity above. Give reasons why you have chosen it.

Third development: _____

_____

_____

_____

Why I have chosen this: _____

_____

_____

_____

Details to support this point: _____

_____

_____

_____

_____

4 The development of the Cold War 2

4.1 The Berlin Crisis, 1948–49

This was the first major crisis of the Cold War.

The division of Germany into zones

- During the peace conferences of 1945 (see pages 4–5), the Allies had agreed to divide both Germany and Berlin into four zones of occupation. Berlin was in Soviet-controlled East Germany. The Western Allies were allowed access to their sectors by road, rail, canal and air.
- Stalin did not want the Allies inside Berlin.
- In 1947, the US and British zones in Berlin merged into one economic unit known as Bizonia.

The Berlin blockade and airlift

- In June 1948, the Western powers announced plans to create a West German state and introduced a new currency, the western Deutschmark.
- On 24 June 1948, Stalin accused the West of interfering in the Soviet zone. He cut off road, rail and canal traffic in an attempt to starve West Berlin.
- Truman was determined to stand up to the Soviet Union and show that he was serious about containment. The only way into Berlin was by air. So the Allies decided to airlift supplies from their bases in West Germany.
- The airlift began on 28 June 1948 and lasted for ten months. It was the start of the biggest airlift in history.
- The airlift reached its peak on 16–17 April 1949 when 1398 flights landed nearly 13,000 tons of supplies in 24 hours.
- By May 1949, Stalin had lifted the **blockade**.

Impact of the blockade and airlift

- It greatly increased East–West rivalry. Truman saw the crisis as a great victory. West Berlin had survived and stood up to the Soviet Union. For Stalin it was a defeat and a humiliation.
- It confirmed the divisions of Germany and Berlin. In May 1949, the Western Allies announced the Federal Republic of Germany (FRG). Stalin's response was rapid and in October 1949 the Soviet zone became the German Democratic Republic (GDR).
- It led to the creation of the North Atlantic Treaty Organization or **NATO**.

4.2 The formation of NATO, 1949

The Berlin Crisis had confirmed Truman's commitment to Western Europe. Western European states, even joined together, were no match for the Soviet Union and needed the formal support of the USA (see map on page 12). In April 1949, the North Atlantic Treaty was signed. NATO's main purpose was to prevent Soviet expansion.

Consequences of the formation of NATO

- The USA was now committed to the defence of Western Europe.
- Stalin believed that NATO was aimed against the Soviet Union.
- Within six years, the Soviet Union set up the Warsaw **Pact** (see page 12).
- Europe was now divided in a state of permanent hostility between the superpowers.

Key terms

Blockade
The surrounding of a place with troops or ships to prevent the entry or exit of supplies

NATO A Western military alliance which was set up after the Berlin Crisis of 1948–49 to protect the freedom and security of its members

Pact A formal agreement between individuals or states

Revision task

Draw a flow chart to show the causes, events and results of the Berlin Crisis of 1948–49.

Exam tips

1 Students often confuse this crisis with the crisis over the Berlin Wall in 1961. An easy way to remember the difference is 'B' for blockade comes before 'W' for wall.

2 Questions on NATO are often not well answered as students fail to revise its features and importance. Ensure you revise these thoroughly.

Develop the detail

Below are an exam-style question and a paragraph which is part of the answer to the question. The paragraph gives the importance of the Potsdam Conference but this is not supported with sufficient evidence. Complete the paragraph by adding more detail about the importance of the Potsdam Conference.

Explain **two** of the following:

- The importance of the Potsdam Conference (1945) for relations between the USA and the Soviet Union.
- The importance of the Truman Doctrine (1947) for relations between the USA and the Soviet Union.
- The importance of the Berlin Crisis (1948–49) for the development of the Cold War.

> The Potsdam Conference was important because it led to differences between the Soviet Union and the USA over Germany. It also led to differences between the two superpowers over what should happen to countries in Eastern Europe.

Spot the mistakes

Below is a paragraph written in answer to the question above. However, the student has made a series of mistakes, some factual and some in how the question is answered. Once you have identified the mistakes, rewrite the paragraph.

> The Truman Doctrine of 1949 was important because it led to American support for the Italian government, which was now able to defeat communism. The USA became committed to a policy of containment and became far more involved in the affairs of Asia. It was also important because it led to the Long telegram, which provided economic aid to Europe.

Now have a go at the third option in the question: the importance of the Berlin Crisis (1948–49) for the development of the Cold War:

- jot down examples of its importance in relation to the given factor
- introduce the first example of its importance in relation to the given factor
- fully explain the example
- introduce the second example of its importance in relation to the given factor
- fully explain the example.

5 The Cold War intensifies 1

The Cold War and East–West rivalry increased even more in the years after the Berlin Crisis.

5.1 The Warsaw Pact, 1955

In 1955, the Soviet Union set up the Warsaw Pact. It was a military alliance of eight nations and was designed to counter the threat of NATO.

Consequences

The existence of two rival alliance systems in the Cold War – in the west NATO and in the east the Warsaw Pact – increased rivalry between the USA and the Soviet Union and intensified the **arms race**.

> **Key term**
>
> **Arms race** A competition between nations for superiority in the development and accumulation of weapons

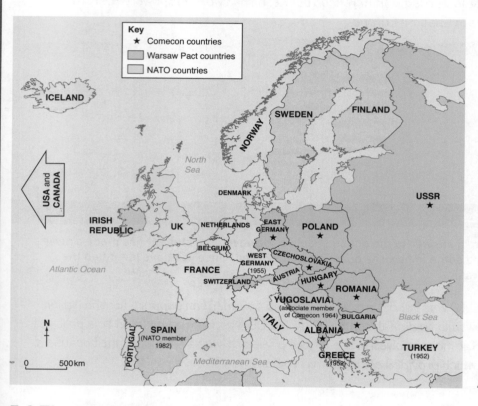

Alliances, 1945–55.

5.2 The arms race

Both superpowers spent more and more money on arms development:

- By 1949, the Soviet Union had developed and tested its own atomic bomb. This was earlier than the USA had expected.
- Now that the USA and the Soviet Union had the atomic bomb, they both began to pour money into projects to build more and bigger bombs.
- Truman ordered a new powerful weapon to be built: the hydrogen or H-bomb.
- In 1953, the Soviet Union tested an H-bomb only a few months after the first US test.
- By 1953, both the USA and the Soviet Union possessed hydrogen bombs.
- Both countries continued to develop bigger and more powerful nuclear weapons.

> **Revision task**
>
> Try coming up with a mnemonic (a pattern of letters, ideas or associations) to help you remember which countries were part of the Warsaw Pact.

The impact of *Sputnik*

- There was hope that the two superpowers would slow down their arms development.
- However, in 1957 the situation changed completely when a Soviet rocket launched *Sputnik*, a satellite which could orbit the earth in one and a half hours.
- The USA saw this launch as a military threat.
- The USA increased its spending on missiles and placed missile bases in some European countries.
- *Sputnik* therefore accelerated the arms programme due to US fears that the Soviet Union was overtaking them in arms development.

 ## Consequences and importance

Having read the information on pages 8, 10 and 12, make a copy of the table below. Explain the consequences and importance of each event for relations between the two superpowers.

Event	Consequences	Importance
The Truman Doctrine		
The Marshall Plan		
Berlin Crisis		
NATO		
Arms race		
Warsaw Pact		

Matching dates and events

- Place the following events in the correct chronological order on the timeline below.
- Give one consequence of each event.

A Truman Doctrine
B Setting up of the Warsaw Pact
C Setting up of NATO
D Potsdam Conference

E Soviet Union tested the H-bomb
F Beginning of the blockade of Berlin
G Long telegram

Year	Event	Consequence
1945		
1946		
1947		
1948		
1949		
1950		
1951		
1952		
1953		
1954		
1955		

6 The Cold War intensifies 2

6.1 The Hungarian uprising, 1956

This further increased rivalry between the USA and the Soviet Union.

Causes

The Soviet Union had established control of Hungary in the years after the Second World War (see page 6). Soviet influence was very unpopular as there was little freedom:

- The Hungarian economy was controlled by the Soviet Union through Comecon. This body prevented Hungary trading with Western Europe and receiving any Marshall Plan aid. Hungary was forced to trade on uneven terms with the Soviet Union. This meant that Hungary did not always receive a fair price for its exports there.

- Mátyás Rákosi from the Hungarian Communist Party led Hungary and used terror and brutality to keep control, killing an estimated 2000 people. The secret police (AVH) became a hated and dreaded part of Hungarian life.

- When Stalin died in 1953, the new leader of the Soviet Union, Malenkov, did not favour Rákosi and replaced him with Imre Nagy. This shows the control that the Soviet Union had in Hungary. However, in April 1955, Nagy was removed and Rákosi returned and resumed his unpopular dictatorship.

> **Key individual**
>
> **Nikita Khrushchev**
> Leader of the Soviet Union from 1955 until 1964. In a 1956 'secret speech', he discussed Stalin's crimes for the first time, starting a process called de-Stalinisation, and later he presided over the Cuban Missile Crisis of 1962

Events

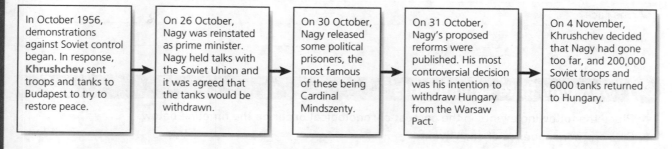

| In October 1956, demonstrations against Soviet control began. In response, **Khrushchev** sent troops and tanks to Budapest to try to restore peace. | On 26 October, Nagy was reinstated as prime minister. Nagy held talks with the Soviet Union and it was agreed that the tanks would be withdrawn. | On 30 October, Nagy released some political prisoners, the most famous of these being Cardinal Mindszenty. | On 31 October, Nagy's proposed reforms were published. His most controversial decision was his intention to withdraw Hungary from the Warsaw Pact. | On 4 November, Khrushchev decided that Nagy had gone too far, and 200,000 Soviet troops and 6000 tanks returned to Hungary. |

The Soviet invasion

- Khrushchev was anxious not to be seen as weak by other members of the Warsaw Pact.

- Khrushchev was afraid that events in Hungary could encourage similar revolts in other Soviet satellite states.

- Furthermore, Mao Zedong, the Chinese leader, was urging him to stand firm against any deviation from communism.

- Khrushchev was able to keep control, and a new Soviet-backed leader, Kádár, was installed. Nagy was arrested and shot in 1958.

6.2 International reaction

- There was very little that the West, especially the USA and Britain, could do to help the Hungarians.

- The West condemned the actions of the Soviet Union, but Hungary was too far away for military intervention.

- The Western powers were keen to avoid military confrontation with the Soviet Union.

- Britain, France and the USA were preoccupied with the Suez Crisis.

> **Revision task**
>
> Draw a timeline for the years 1945–56. On the timeline include the key events of the Cold War.

> **Exam tip**
>
> The events of 1956 in Hungary are complicated. Ensure you have a thorough understanding of the chronology of that year.

Memory map

Use the information on the opposite page to create a memory map about the key features of the Hungarian uprising of 1956. Your diagram should include the reasons for the Soviet invasion, the events of the invasion, its importance and consequences.

 You're the examiner

Below is an exam-style question.

Write a narrative account analysing the key events which increased rivalry between the two superpowers in the years 1949–56.

> **You may use the following information in your answer:**
> - NATO (1949)
> - The Hungarian Crisis (1956)
>
> You **must** also use information of your own.

1 Below are a mark scheme and a paragraph which is part of an answer to the question. Read the paragraph and the mark scheme. Decide which level you would award the paragraph. Write the level below, along with a justification for your choice.

Mark scheme

Level	Mark	
1	1–2	A simple or generalised narrative is provided, showing limited development, organisation of material and limited knowledge and understanding of the events included
2	3–5	A narrative is given showing some organisation of material into a sequence of events leading to an outcome. The account shows some analysis of the linkage between them but some of the passages may lack coherence and organisation
		Accurate and relevant knowledge is added, showing some knowledge and understanding of the events.
		Maximum 4 marks for answers that do not go beyond aspects prompted by the stimulus points
3	6–8	A narrative is given which organises material into a clear sequence of events leading to an outcome. The account of the events analyses the linkage between them and is coherent and logically structured
		Accurate and relevant knowledge is included, showing good knowledge and understanding of the key features or characteristics of the events
		No access to Level 3 for answers that do not go beyond aspects prompted by the stimulus points

STUDENT ANSWER

In April 1949, the North Atlantic Treaty was signed. Although a defensive alliance, NATO's main purpose was to prevent Soviet expansion. The USA was now committed to the defence of Western Europe. Stalin did not believe it was a defensive alliance. He believed it was aimed against the Soviet Union. In 1956, the Soviet Union invaded Hungary. Khrushchev did not want to be seen as weak by other members of the Warsaw Pact. He was afraid that events in Hungary could encourage similar revolts in other Soviet satellite states. There was very little that the West, especially the USA and Britain, could do, apart from condemn the actions of the Soviet Union, to help the Hungarians.

Level ☐   Reason _____

_____

2 Now suggest what the student has to do with this paragraph to achieve the next level.

_____

3 Try and rewrite this paragraph at a higher level.

Key topic 2 Cold War crises, 1958–70

In the 1960s there were three major crises in the Cold War. Each one greatly increased tension between the superpowers. The first was in 1961 when the Soviet Union constructed the Berlin Wall separating East Berlin from West Berlin. The following year the two superpowers were on the brink of nuclear war due to the Cuban Missile Crisis. The third crisis was in 1968 and was due to developments in Czechoslovakia.

1 Increased tension over Berlin, 1958–61

REVISED ☐

The Soviet Union's desire to remove the Western Allies from Berlin created a crisis in 1961.

1.1 Problems in East Germany

Even after 1949, Berlin continued to pose a problem for the USA and Soviet Union:

- Between 1949 and 1961, about 4 million East Germans fled to the West through Berlin. Khrushchev wanted the removal of the Allies because West Berlin was an area of capitalist prosperity and symbolised the success of Western Europe within communist territory.

- The Soviet Union also claimed that the USA and its Allies used West Berlin as a base for espionage.

The Berlin Ultimatum

In 1958, Khrushchev issued the Berlin **Ultimatum**. He accused the Allies of breaking the Potsdam Agreement, and told them that they should leave Berlin within six months. The US president, Eisenhower, seemed prepared to negotiate. He did not want to risk a war over Berlin.

Summit meetings, 1959–61

- In May 1959, the Geneva Summit of Foreign Ministers failed to reach agreement on the problem of Berlin.

- In September 1959, Khrushchev visited the USA to attend a summit meeting at Camp David. Disarmament was discussed and they agreed on a further summit meeting over Berlin.

- Khrushchev and Eisenhower were set to meet in Paris on 14 May 1960. Nine days before the **summit conference** was due to open, the Soviet Union announced that it had shot down an American U-2 spy plane near the city of Sverdlovsk. The pilot was captured and put on trial.

- Khrushchev demanded that all such flights stop and that the USA apologise for spying. Eisenhower would not and Khrushchev stormed out of the first session.

- At the Vienna summit of June 1961, Khrushchev again demanded that Western forces leave West Berlin. The new US president, **Kennedy**, refused.

1.2 The Berlin Wall, 1961

The differences over Berlin worsened in 1961 with the building of the Berlin Wall:

- On 13 August 1961, Khrushchev closed the border between East and West Berlin. East German troops and workers installed barbed-wire entanglements and fences.

- The USA and its Allies did nothing to stop the building of a wall.

- Over time, East German officials replaced the makeshift wall with one that was sturdier and more difficult to scale.

Key terms

Summit conference A meeting of heads of state or government, usually with considerable media exposure and tight security

Ultimatum A final demand or statement of terms, the rejection of which will result in retaliation or a breakdown in relations

Key individual

John F. Kennedy Won the US presidential election of 1960 and was the US leader during the Berlin Crisis of 1961 and the Cuban Missile Crisis of 1962. He was determined to get tough with communism but his presidency was short-lived as he was assassinated in 1963

Revision task

Prioritise the consequences of the events of the early 1960s in Berlin.

Exam tip

Ensure you do not confuse the events of 1961 with the Berlin Crisis of 1948–49.

Consequences

- Peace was maintained, but at a price for the German people. Families were split, and travel restrictions made it very difficult for relatives to see one another.
- The construction of the Berlin Wall led to a serious stand-off between the two superpowers.
- President Kennedy worked behind the scenes to avoid conflict. He promised Khrushchev that if the Soviet Union removed its troops, the USA would do the same. This ended the stand-off.
- The flow of refugees was stopped.
- President Kennedy visited West Germany in 1963. He declared that the city was a symbol of the struggle between the forces of freedom and the communist world and coined the famous phrase 'Ich bin ein Berliner' ('I am a Berliner').

 Identifying consequences

Below is an exam-style question.

Explain two consequences of the Berlin Crisis of 1961.

In answering this question, it is important that you focus on consequence. In the table below are statements about the Berlin Crisis. Identify (with a tick in the appropriate column) whether they are causes, events or consequences of the Berlin Crisis.

Statement	Cause	Event	Consequence
The flow of refugees was stopped. It led to the Cuban Missile Crisis of 1962			
On 13 August 1961, Khrushchev closed the border between East and West Berlin			
The construction of the Berlin Wall led to a serious stand-off between the two superpowers			
Between 1949 and 1961, about 4 million East Germans fled to the West through Berlin			
The East German officials replaced the makeshift wall with one that was sturdier and more difficult to scale			
It led to the Cuban Missile Crisis of 1962			
East German troops and workers installed barbed-wire entanglements and fences			
The Soviet Union claimed that the USA and its Allies used West Berlin as a base for espionage			

 How important

Here is an exam-style question:

Explain the importance of the Berlin Crisis (1961) for the development of the Cold War.

Below is a table showing the importance of the Berlin Crisis. Copy and complete the table by:
- making a decision about how important each factor was in the development of the Cold War
- briefly explaining each decision.

Factor	Very important	Important	Quite important
Berlin Wall			
The Paris Summit, 1960			
Kennedy's visit to Berlin			

2 The Cuban Missile Crisis

The Cuban Missile Crisis was the most serious crisis of the Cold War, with the two superpowers close to nuclear war.

2.1 Increased tension over Cuba

- The USA had strong economic interests in Cuba and controlled most of Cuba's industry, railways and electricity production.
- In 1959, Fidel Castro led a successful revolution against the unpopular and repressive military dictator of Cuba, General Batista, who had been under the influence of the USA.
- Castro wanted greater independence from the USA and took all American property that was located in Cuba. In response, the USA banned the import of Cuban sugar, which threatened to bankrupt the Cuban economy.
- The USA, aware that Castro had some connections to communism, refused to acknowledge his government. Castro removed US influence from Cuba and moved closer to the Soviet Union. The Soviet Union offered to buy Cuban sugar and to provide machinery and technological help.

The Bay of Pigs incident

- In 1961, the USA organised an attempt to overthrow Castro, known as the Bay of Pigs invasion. This was a total failure for President Kennedy. The **CIA** had been convinced that the Cuban people would revolt against Castro. However, they underestimated his popularity and there was no uprising.
- As a result of this failure, Castro grew closer to the Soviet leader, Khrushchev, and, in May 1962, agreed to station Soviet nuclear weapons on Cuba. On 14 October, an American U–2 spy plane took photos revealing that missile sites were being built.

> **Key term**
>
> **CIA** Central Intelligence Agency: the arm of the US government tasked with espionage and intelligence activities

> **Revision task**
>
> Draw a table which includes the USA, the Soviet Union and Cuba. In the table, explain what each country gained from the Cuban Missile Crisis. Which country do you think gained the most from the crisis?

> **Exam tip**
>
> The Cuban Missile Crisis is a popular exam topic. Ensure you thoroughly revise the causes, events and results.

2.2 Events of the Cuban Missile Crisis

Days in October 1962	Events
16	Kennedy was told that Khrushchev intended to build missile sites in Cuba
18–19	Kennedy held talks with his closest advisers. The 'Hawks' wanted an aggressive policy, while the 'Doves' favoured a peaceful solution
20	Kennedy decided to impose a naval blockade around Cuba to prevent Soviet missiles and equipment reaching Cuba. The Americans searched any ship suspected of carrying arms or missiles
21	Kennedy made a broadcast to the American people, informing them of the potential threat and what he intended to do
23	Khrushchev sent a letter to Kennedy insisting that Soviet ships would force their way through the blockade
24	Khrushchev issued a statement insisting that the Soviet Union would use nuclear weapons in the event of a war
25	Kennedy wrote to Khrushchev asking him to withdraw missiles from Cuba
26	Khrushchev replied to Kennedy's letter. He said he would withdraw the missiles if the USA promised not to invade Cuba and to withdraw its missiles from Turkey
27	A US spy plane was shot down over Cuba. Attorney General Robert Kennedy (brother of the president) proposed a deal with the Soviet Union. The USA would withdraw missiles from Turkey as long as it was kept secret
28	Khrushchev accepted the deal

Consequences

The superpowers had almost gone to war: a war that would have destroyed much of the world. However, the crisis did lead to better relations:

- The 'hotline': to ensure that the two leaders could communicate more quickly and directly, a hotline telephone link was established between the White House and the Kremlin.
- The Limited Test Ban Treaty, 1963: both the USA and the Soviet Union agreed to stop testing nuclear weapons above ground and underwater.
- The Outer Space Treaty 1967: the two superpowers, together with Britain and several other countries promised to use outer space for peaceful purposes and not to place nuclear weapons in orbit.
- The Nuclear Non-proliferation Treaty, 1968: this was designed to stop the spread of nuclear weapons.
- Relations between the two superpowers also improved with the USA selling grain to the Soviet Union.

 You're the examiner

Below is an exam-style question.

Write a narrative account analysing the key events of 1959–62 which led to the Cuban Missile Crisis (1962).

You may use the following information in your answer.

- Castro becomes leader
- The Bay of Pigs invasion (1961)

You **must** also use information of your own.

1 Below is a paragraph which is part of an answer to the question. Read the paragraph and use the mark scheme on page 15. Decide which level you would award the paragraph. Write the level below, along with a justification for your choice.

STUDENT ANSWER

Castro removed American influence from Cuba and moved closer to the Soviet Union. Khrushchev and the Soviet Union increased their influence in Cuba when they offered to buy Cuban sugar and to provide machinery and technological help. In 1959, Castro had led a successful revolution against the military dictator of Cuba, General Batista, who had been very much under the influence of America. The USA did not like Castro and the influence of the Soviet Union in Cuba. The USA organised an attempt to overthrow Castro, known as the Bay of Pigs invasion, to remove Castro. This failed because the CIA had been convinced that the Cuban people would revolt against Castro but they did not. The Cuban Missile Crisis then started.

Level [ ]   Reason _____

2 Now suggest what the student has to do to achieve a higher level.

_____

_____

3 Try and rewrite this paragraph at a higher level.

3 The Soviet invasion of Czechoslovakia, 1968

This severely tested closer relations between the superpowers.

3.1 Increased tension over Czechoslovakia

In the 1960s there was growing opposition to Soviet control for several reasons:

- Antonín Novotný had been the Czech leader since 1957. He was unpopular because he was a hardline communist who refused to introduce reform.
- The Czech economy was in serious decline in the 1960s. This led to a fall in the standard of living. Novotný's attempts at economic reform were unsuccessful.
- Many Czechs began to demand greater democracy, including **Alexander Dubček**.

3.2 The Prague Spring

The 'Prague Spring' refers to a series of reforms introduced by Dubček in the spring of 1968. The reforms included:

- Greater political freedom including free speech and the abolition of press censorship.
- The powers of the secret police to arrest without trial were reduced.
- Travel restrictions were removed and fresh contact was made with the West, such as trade with West Germany.
- More power to regional governments and to the Czech parliament.
- The introduction of elements of capitalism in the economy.
- The production of new literature supporting the changes.
- The creation of works councils representing the workforce to improve working conditions in factories and increased rights for trade unions.
- A ten-year programme for political change which would bring about democratic elections, and create a new form of democratic socialism.

Dubček's reforms, however, encouraged the growth of opposition to communism and demands for even more radical reforms.

3.3 Re-establishing Soviet control

The Soviet Union was suspicious of the changes taking place in Czechoslovakia:

- **Brezhnev** was worried that Czechoslovakia might leave the Warsaw Pact and that NATO might move in.
- Brezhnev came under pressure from the East German leader, Walter Ulbricht, and the Polish leader, Gomułka, to stop reform in Czechoslovakia.

Key features of invasion

- On 20–21 August 1968, thousands of Warsaw Pact troops entered Czechoslovakia.
- Czechs threw petrol bombs at the Soviet tanks as they moved through Prague. Buildings were set on fire and protesters assembled in Wenceslas Square.
- Dubček and the other leaders were arrested and taken to Moscow, and forced to accept the end of the Czech moves towards democracy.

Key individuals

Leonid Brezhnev
Succeeded Khrushchev as leader of the Soviet Union in 1964. He remained as leader until his death in 1982. He supported the policy of *détente* and ordered the invasion of Afghanistan in 1979, which ended this policy and led to the Second Cold War

Alexander Dubček
A Slovak politician and, briefly, leader of Czechoslovakia. He attempted to reform the Communist regime during the Prague Spring of 1968 but he was forced to resign following the Warsaw Pact invasion of Czechoslovakia. In 1969 he was removed as leader. He was killed in a car accident in 1992

Revision task

Place the following events in chronological order:

- Soviet invasion of Czechoslovakia
- Jan Palach set himself on fire
- Prague Spring
- Brezhnev Doctrine.

Give a brief explanation of the importance of each.

Exam tip

You may well be asked to explain key developments in Czechoslovakia in 1968 or the consequences of the Soviet invasion. Ensure you thoroughly revise this crisis.

Consequences of Soviet invasion

States	Consequence
Czechoslovakia	Demonstrations against the Soviet invasion went on until April 1969. In January 1969, Jan Palach, a student, set fire to himself in Wenceslas Square to protest against the Soviet invasion
Soviet Union	It gave rise to the Brezhnev Doctrine. This redefined communism as a one-party state where all member countries had to remain part of the Warsaw Pact. It also sent out a message to the members of the Warsaw Pact that the Soviet Union would suppress any attempt to relax Communist control
Warsaw Pact states	Some Communist countries began to move away from Moscow. President Ceausescu of Romania refused to send troops to join the forces invading Czechoslovakia

3.4 International reaction

The Soviet invasion temporarily worsened relations between East and West. The West, especially Britain and the USA, protested at Soviet actions. The USA did nothing else because they were preoccupied with the war in Vietnam.

Western European countries followed the USA's lead – they condemned the invasion but provided no military help. Western European Communist parties in Italy and France were outraged by the Soviet invasion.

Relevance

Below are an exam-style question and a series of statements on the Soviet invasion of Czechoslovakia. Decide which statements are:

- relevant to the question (R)
- partially relevant to the question (PR)
- irrelevant to the question (I).

Tick the appropriate column.

Explain two consequences of the Soviet invasion of Czechoslovakia (1968).

Statements	R	PR	I
The Soviet invasion temporarily worsened relations between East and West			
In the 1960s, there was growing opposition to Soviet control of Czechoslovakia			
Western European countries condemned the invasion but provided no military help			
Some Communists, including Ceausescu of Romania, began to move away from Moscow			
On 20–21 August 1968, hundreds and thousands of Warsaw Pact troops entered Czechoslovakia			
Czechs threw petrol bombs at the Soviet tanks as they moved through Prague			
Novotný had been the Czech leader since 1957 and was unpopular because he was a hardline Communist			
It gave rise to the Brezhnev Doctrine. This redefined communism as a one-party state			
Many Czechs began to demand greater democracy, including Dubček			
During the Soviet invasion, buildings were set on fire and protesters assembled in Wenceslas Square			
The 'Prague Spring' refers to a series of reforms introduced by Dubček in the spring of 1968			
In January 1969, Jan Palach, a student, set fire to himself in Wenceslas Square to protest against the Soviet invasion			

Now write an answer to this question.

Cold War relations changed greatly during these years. During the 1970s, the policy of *détente* improved East–West relations. However, the Soviet Union's invasion of Afghanistan in 1979 brought about the Second Cold War. By 1989, the leaders of the USA and the Soviet Union had announced that the Cold War was over.

1 Attempts to reduce tension between East and West 1

REVISED

After the Cuban Missile Crisis there was a move to improve relations and relax tension between the USA and Soviet Union. This became known as *détente* or a policy of **thaw**.

1.1 *Détente* in the 1970s

Détente emerged due to developments in the late 1960s and early 1970s:

- The threat of a nuclear war during the Cuban Missile Crisis had had a sobering effect on all concerned.
- Both the USA and the Soviet Union were keen on arms limitation talks in order to reduce their ever-increasing defence spending.
- By 1968, the USA was seeking to end the war. After **Richard Nixon** became president, it was hoped that if the USA improved trade and technology links and made an offer of arms reduction, then Brezhnev might persuade his North Vietnamese ally to negotiate an end to the war. The idea of offering concessions was called 'linkage' by Nixon's advisers.
- Nixon had visited China three months earlier and Brezhnev did not want to see a Chinese–US alliance develop. The Soviet leader was keen to gain access to US technology and further grain sales.

1.2 SALT 1

The Strategic Arms Limitation Talks (**SALT** 1) began in 1969 and were completed in May 1972:

- The two superpowers agreed that there would be no further production of strategic **ballistic** missiles (short-range, lightweight missiles).
- Both powers agreed that submarines carrying nuclear weapons would only be introduced when existing stocks of intercontinental ballistic missiles (ICBMs) became obsolete.

SALT 1 was significant because it was the first agreement between the superpowers that successfully limited the number of nuclear weapons they held.

1.3 The Helsinki Agreements

These were signed in 1975. The USA and the USSR, along with 33 other nations, made declarations about three distinct international issues (called 'baskets' by the signatories).

Security	Cooperation	Human rights
Recognition of Europe's frontiers The Soviet Union accepted the existence of West Germany	There was a call for closer economic, scientific and cultural links – these would lead to even closer political agreement	Each signatory agreed to respect human rights and basic freedoms such as thought, speech, religion and freedom from unfair arrest

Key terms

Ballistic The flight of an object through space, such as rockets that are fired from weapons. A ballistic missile is guided only when it is first launched

Détente The relaxing of tension or hostility between nations

SALT Strategic Arms Limitation Talks: attempts by the USA and the Soviet Union to agree to limit the arms race

Thaw A period of improved relations between East and West

Key individual

Richard Nixon Served as US president from 1969 until his resignation in 1974. He was responsible for improved relations with both China and the Soviet Union

Exam tip

Détente is the least well-known period of the Cold War. Ensure you know what it means and its key features.

1.4 SALT 2

SALT 2 began in 1974 and the treaty was signed in June 1979. The terms were:

- A limit of 2400 strategic nuclear delivery vehicles for each side.
- A limit of 1320 multiple independently targetable re-entry vehicle (MIRV) systems for each side.
- A ban on the construction of new land-based ICBM launchers.
- The agreement would last until 1985.

However, the US Senate refused to ratify the SALT 2 agreements following the Soviet invasion of Afghanistan in December 1979 (see page 26).

(see page 26)

Revision task

How did the following improve relations between the superpowers?

- SALT 1
- the Helsinki Agreements
- SALT 2.

Organising knowledge

Use the information on pages 22–23 to complete the table below to summarise the key features of *détente*.

Meaning of *détente*	
SALT 1	
Helsinki Agreements	
SALT 2	

Linking events

Below are an exam-style question and a series of statements:

- Place the statements in the correct sequence.
- Show links between the events. You could use link phrases such as 'this led to', 'as a result of this'.

You may use the following information in your answer:

- SALT 1 (1971)
- Helsinki Agreements (1975)

You **must** also use information of your own.

Write a narrative account analysing the key events of *détente* in the 1970s.

Statement	Order	Linking statements
The Helsinki Agreements were signed in 1975. The USA and the Soviet Union, along with 33 other nations, made declarations about three distinct international issues		
The Strategic Arms Limitation Talks began in 1969 and were completed three years later		
Each signatory at Helsinki agreed to respect human rights and basic freedoms such as thought, speech, religion and freedom from unfair arrest		
SALT 2 was signed in June 1979. However, the US Senate refused to ratify the SALT 2 agreements following the Soviet invasion of Afghanistan in December 1979		
In 1975 there was a joint space mission in which an American Apollo spacecraft and a Soviet Soyuz spacecraft docked high above Earth. This marked the beginning of superpower cooperation in space		
The two superpowers agreed that there would be no further production of strategic ballistic missiles and that submarines carrying nuclear weapons would only be introduced when existing stocks of intercontinental ballistic missiles became obsolete		
At Helsinki there was a recognition of Europe's frontiers. The Soviet Union accepted the existence of West Germany		

2 Attempts to reduce tension between East and West 2

2.1 Gorbachev's 'new thinking'

Mikhail Gorbachev was the last leader of the Soviet Union and was prepared to adopt drastic policies to improve superpower relations. He had to attempt to improve the relationship, as he knew that, without change, the Soviet Union would collapse.

Gorbachev's 'new thinking' involved three important strategies which greatly changed relationships with the West:

- he initiated sweeping reforms in the Communist Party and Soviet system in the USSR:
  - *perestroika* (restructuring) included economic reforms designed to make the Soviet economy more efficient
  - *glasnost* (openness) ensured censorship of the press was relaxed
- he ended the arms race with the USA and signed various arms reduction agreements
- he stopped Soviet interference in Eastern European satellite states such as Poland and Czechoslovakia.

2.2 The summit conferences

A series of summit meetings took place in the years 1985–90 to discuss arms limitations.

Meeting	Result
Geneva, November 1985	Although nothing was decided, the Geneva Accord was set out which committed the USA and Soviet Union to speed up arms talks. Both Gorbachev and US President **Ronald Reagan** promised to meet in the near future. It was clear to many observers that the two men had got on well
Reykjavík, 1986	The leaders failed to reach agreement on arms limitation
Washington, December 1987	This was more successful and the **Intermediate Nuclear Forces (INF) Treaty** was signed (see below)
Washington, 1990	President Bush and Gorbachev agreed on the Treaty for the Reduction and Limitation of Strategic Arms (START) in which they agreed to reduce their strategic forces over seven years

2.3 The INF Treaty, 1987

- The INF Treaty eliminated nuclear and conventional ground-launched ballistic and cruise missiles with ranges of 500–5500 kilometres (300–3400 miles). By the treaty's deadline, 1 June 1991, a total of 2692 of such weapons had been destroyed, 846 by the USA and 1846 by the Soviet Union.
- Also under the treaty, both nations were allowed to inspect each other's military installations.
- It was the first treaty to reduce the number of nuclear missiles that the superpowers possessed. It therefore went much further than SALT 1 (see page 22), which simply limited the growth of Soviet and US stockpiles.

Key individuals

Mikhail Gorbachev Served as leader of the Soviet Union from 1985 until 1991. During this period he reformed the Soviet Union through his policies of *glasnost* and *perestroika*, improved relations with the USA and was mainly responsible for the ending of the Cold War

Ronald Reagan Served as US president from 1981 to 1989. At first he was determined to 'get tough' with the Soviet Union and communism but this approach softened in the later 1980s due to closer relations with Gorbachev

Key term

Intermediate-Range Nuclear Forces (INF) Treaty A treaty between the USA and the Soviet Union for the elimination of their intermediate- and short-range missiles.

Revision task

Put the following key developments in chronological order:

- Reykjavík summit
- INF
- Geneva summit.

Give a brief explanation of the importance of each for the Cold War.

Exam tip

You will not need detailed knowledge of Gorbachev's policies in the Soviet Union but an understanding of how they affected relations with the USA

Memory map

Use the information on page 24 to add details to the diagram below about the consequences and importance of Gorbachev's new thinking, the summit conferences and the INF.

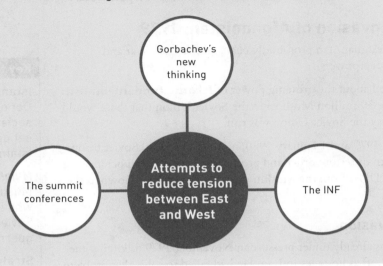

Gorbachev's new thinking

Attempts to reduce tension between East and West

The summit conferences

The INF

Concentric circles

In the concentric circles below, rank order the importance of the summit conferences of the later 1980s and early 1990s for the Cold War, beginning with the most important in the middle to the least important on the outside. Explain your decisions.

- Geneva, 1985
- Reykjavík, 1986
- Washington, 1987
- Washington, 1990.

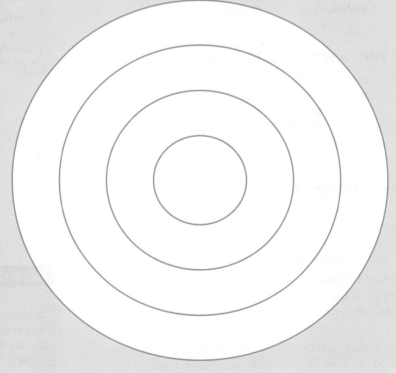

3 Flashpoints

The attempts at *détente* in the 1970s had been quite serious, but there were a number of flashpoints in the world where the superpowers were at loggerheads.

3.1 The Soviet invasion of Afghanistan, 1979

The Soviet invasion of Afghanistan profoundly changed the Cold War and relations between the superpowers.

Brezhnev was concerned about the growing power of **Islamic fundamentalism** and wanted to show the 30 million Muslims in the Soviet Union that there would be no changes in the way the Soviet Union was run.

Between 25 December 1979 and 1 January 1980, more than 50,000 Soviet troops were sent to Afghanistan to restore order and protect the People's Democratic Party of Afghanistan (PDPA) from the Muslim guerrilla movement known as the *mujahideen*.

Significance of invasion

US President Carter was already under pressure in November 1979 following the seizure of US embassy staff as hostages in Iran. He had failed to solve that problem by the end of the year, and some in the USA were accusing him of being a weak leader. He therefore made a firm approach with the Soviet Union over the invasion:

- The Carter Doctrine stated that the USA would use military force if necessary to defend its national interests, especially oil interests, in the Persian Gulf region. It also promised US military aid to all the countries bordering Afghanistan.
- The tough line was continued when Carter asked the Senate not to ratify the SALT 2 treaty.
- Carter pressured the US Olympic Committee to boycott the Moscow Olympic Games of 1980. Sixty-one other countries followed the USA's example.
- The Soviet Union retaliated four years later by boycotting the Los Angeles Olympic Games.

3.2 Reagan and the 'Second Cold War'

Reagan, who defeated Carter in the 1980 presidential election, believed in taking a far tougher line with the Soviet Union than Carter. Reagan had no interest in *détente* and was prepared to confront the Soviet Union whenever possible. He described the Soviet Union as the 'evil empire'. The US Congress agreed to Reagan's demand for increased defence spending, which would cost more than a trillion dollars in the years 1981–87.

The Strategic Defence Initiative (SDI)

- Reagan's plan was to launch an army of satellites equipped with powerful lasers which could intercept Soviet missiles in space and destroy them before they could do any harm to the USA. He believed that 'Star Wars' technology would make Soviet nuclear missiles useless and force the USSR to disarm.
- The **Strategic Defence Initiative (SDI)** proved to be a turning point in the arms race. During *détente*, the superpowers had been evenly matched and had worked together to limit the growth of nuclear stockpiles. SDI was a complete break from this policy.
- Soviet leaders knew that they could not compete with Reagan's 'Star Wars' plan. They were behind the USA in space and computer technology and the Soviet economy was not producing enough wealth to fund even more defence spending.

> ### Key terms
>
> **Islamic fundamentalism** Opposes secular Western society and seeks to set up a state based on Islamic law
>
> ***Mujahideen*** Afghan Muslim freedom fighters who fought against the Soviet occupation using guerrilla tactics
>
> **Strategic Defence Initiative (SDI)** Also known as 'Star Wars', the plan was to develop a sophisticated anti-ballistic missile system in order to prevent missile attacks from other countries, specifically the Soviet Union

> ### Revision task
>
> Summarise in no more than ten words the significance of the Soviet invasion of Afghanistan.

> ### Exam tip
>
> The Soviet invasion of Afghanistan is a very important turning point in the Cold War. Ensure you have thorough knowledge of its features and significance.

RAG: Rate the timeline

Below are an exam-style question and a timeline. Read the question, study the timeline and, using three coloured pens, put a **red**, amber or **green** star next to the events to show:

Red: events and policies that have **no** relevance to the question

Amber: events and policies that have **some** significance to the question

Green: events and policies that have **direct** relevance to the question

Explain **two** of the following:

● The importance of the invasion of Afghanistan (1979) for relations between the USA and the Soviet Union.

● The importance of the SDI for relations between the USA and the Soviet Union.

● The importance of the Olympic Games of 1980 and 1984 for relations between the USA and the Soviet Union.

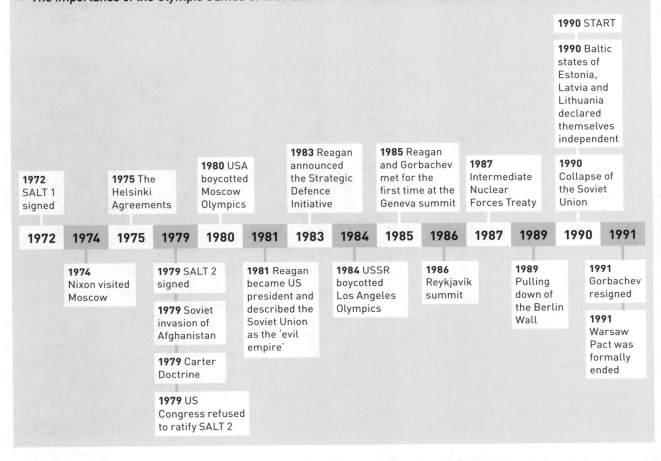

Develop the detail

Below is part of an answer to the first option in the question above. The paragraph contains a limited amount of detail. Annotate the paragraph to add additional detail to the answer.

The invasion of Afghanistan was important because it ended the period of *détente* and increased rivalry between the Soviet Union and the USA. It was important because it led to the Carter Doctrine. It was also important because it led to the USA boycotting the Moscow Olympics of 1980.

4 The collapse of Soviet control of Eastern Europe 1

In the Soviet Union, Gorbachev's reforms (see page 24) encouraged criticism and eventually the downfall of Gorbachev, as well as the break-up of the Soviet Union and the end of the Warsaw Pact.

4.1 The impact of Gorbachev's 'new thinking' on Eastern Europe

The Soviet economy could no longer stand the strain of supporting forces in Eastern Europe.

In 1988, Gorbachev rejected the Brezhnev Doctrine and in 1989 he accepted that members of the Warsaw Pact could make changes to their own countries without expecting outside interference. This became known as the Sinatra Doctrine.

1988: strikes throughout the country

1989: free trade union – Solidarity – won elections. Mazowiecki became the first non-Communist prime minister in Eastern Europe

October 1989: Gorbachev visited East Germany and told them that Soviet troops would not put down East German demonstrations

23 October: 300,000 protested in Leipzig

4 November: 1 million protested in East Berlin

9 November: Berlin Wall pulled down

1991: Germany reunified as one country

'The Velvet Revolution': a bloodless revolution that brought about the overthrow of the Communist government

17 November 1989: huge demonstrations against communism

24 November 1989: Communist government resigned

9 December 1989: Havel became the first non-Communist Czech president since 1948

1990: democratic elections won by Civic Forum – an alliance of non-Communist groups

1988: Gorbachev accepted that Hungary could become a multi-party state

1989: democratic elections won by Democratic Forum, an alliance of non-Communist groups

21 October 1989: the opening of Hungary's borders to East Germans and the West

1990: democratic elections won by renamed Communist Party

16 December 1989: secret police fired on demonstrators

21 December 1989: huge crowd in Bucharest booed President Ceausescu who fled but was later captured

1990: democratic elections won by National Salvation Front containing many non-Communists

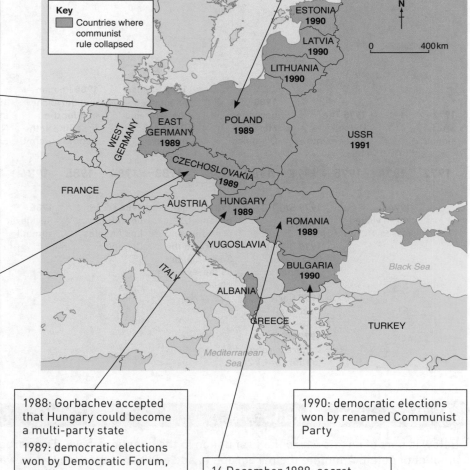

Organising knowledge

Use the information on page 28 to complete the table below to show developments in each country in the years 1988–91 as a result of Gorbachev's new thinking and their importance.

State	Developments	Importance
Poland		
Czechoslovakia		
East Germany		
Romania		
Bulgaria		
Hungary		

Venn diagram

Complete the Venn diagram below showing the consequences of Gorbachev's policies for:

- the Soviet Union
- Eastern Europe
- the Cold War.

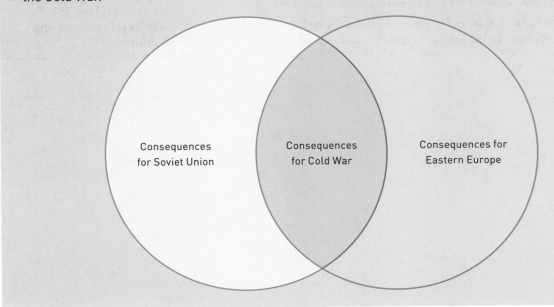

Consequences for Soviet Union

Consequences for Cold War

Consequences for Eastern Europe

5 The collapse of Soviet control of Eastern Europe 2

5.1 The fall of the Berlin Wall

- On 9 November 1989, the East German government announced the opening of the border crossings into West Germany. The people began to dismantle the Berlin Wall.

- Within a few days, over 1 million people had seized the chance to see relatives and experience life in West Germany. West and East Germany were formally reunited in October 1990.

5.2 The collapse of the Soviet Union

- Events in Eastern Europe had a catastrophic impact on the Soviet Union. The many nationalities and ethnic groups saw how the satellite states had been able to break away from Moscow.

- In 1990, the Baltic states of Estonia, Latvia and Lithuania declared themselves independent, which was accepted by Moscow in 1991. This led to other demands for independence within the Soviet Union.

- Gorbachev found that he was opposed by most sections of Soviet society. In August 1991, there was an attempted *coup d'état* which was defeated by Boris Yeltsin, who was president of the Russian Socialist Republic. Gorbachev was restored but he had lost his authority. Gorbachev resigned in December 1991 and the Soviet Union split into several independent states. Now there was only one superpower left – the USA.

> **Key term**
>
> *Coup d'état* Armed rebellion or revolt against the existing government

5.3 The end of the Warsaw Pact and Cold War

In 1989, US President Bush had declared at the Malta Conference that the Cold War was over. However, communism was still undefeated and the Russian coup of August 1991 which overthrew Gorbachev could well have revived rivalry with the West.

- As Soviet control of Eastern Europe fell away, it became obvious that the Warsaw Pact could not survive.

- First Poland, then Hungary and finally East Germany all rejected communism and the Pact no longer served any purpose. Military cooperation stopped in early 1990 and the Warsaw Pact was formally ended in July 1991.

- The fall of the Soviet Union in December 1991 finally ended the rivalry between communism in the East and capitalism in the West.

> **Revision task**
>
> Explain why Gorbachev was so liked and so hated at the same time.

> **Exam tip**
>
> Events in Eastern Europe and the Soviet Union, 1988–91, are complicated. Make sure you understand the key developments and features.

Complete the paragraph

Below are an exam-style question and a paragraph which is part of an answer to this question. Complete the paragraph by providing a further explanation about each consequence.

Explain two consequences of the collapse of the Soviet Union.

> One consequence of the collapse of the Soviet Union was the ending of the Cold War. A second consequence was the break-up of the Soviet Union.

How important

Complete the table below.

● Briefly summarise the importance of each factor in bringing an end to the Cold War.
● Make a decision about the importance of each factor in bringing an end to the Cold War. Give a brief explanation for each choice.

Factor	Key features	Decisive/Important/Quite important
Gorbachev's 'new thinking'		
Summit conferences		
Fall of the Berlin Wall		
INF		
Collapse of the Soviet Union		

Exam focus

Your History GCSE is made up of three exams:

- Paper 1 on a thematic study and historic environment.
- Paper 2 on a British depth study and a period study, in your case Superpower relations and the Cold War, 1941–91.
- Paper 3 on a modern depth study.

For the period study on Paper 2 you have to answer the following types of questions. Each requires you to demonstrate different historical skills:

- **Question 1** is a consequence question in which you have to explain two consequences of a given development or event.

- **Question 2** is a narrative question. You have to write an account which analyses events or developments during a given period in the Cold War and support each with detail. You can choose to write about the two given events, but you must also write about an event or development of your own.

- **Question 3** is an importance question. You are asked to make a judgement on the importance of two different events/developments, supported by a precise and developed explanation.

The table below gives a summary of the question types for Paper 2 and what you need to do.

Question number	Marks	Key words	You need to ...
1	8	Explain **two** consequences of	• Ensure you focus on consequence • Fully explain each consequence
2	8	Write a narrative account analysing ... You may use the following in your answer: [two given events/developments]. You **must** also use information of your own	• Analyse at least three events/developments • Fully explain each with supporting detail
3	16	Explain **two** of the following: • The importance of ... for the ... • The importance of ... for the ... • The importance of ... for the ...	• Choose two of the three developments • Ensure that you focus on importance • Fully explain its importance using precise evidence

Question 1: Consequence

Below is an example exam-style consequence question. It is worth 8 marks.

Explain two consequences of Gorbachev's 'new thinking'.

How to answer

- Underline key points in the question. This will ensure that you focus sharply on what is required.
- Identify two consequences of Gorbachev's 'new thinking'.
- Begin each paragraph by stating the consequence. For example, 'One consequence of Gorbachev's "new thinking" was ... .'

- Give a fully developed explanation about the consequence including precise details.
- State the second consequence. For example, 'A further consequence of Gorbachev's "new thinking" was ...'.
- Give a fully developed explanation about the second consequence including precise evidence.

Quick quizzes at **www.hoddereducation.co.uk/myrevisionnotes**

Below is a sample answer to another exam-style consequence question with comments around it.

Explain two consequences of the Berlin Crisis of 1948–49.

One consequence of the Berlin Crisis of 1948–49 was that it greatly increased East–West rivalry. This was because Truman saw the crisis as a great victory. The Berlin airlift had been very effective in ensuring that supplies reached West Berlin. This reached its peak on 16–17 April 1949 when 1398 flights landed nearly 13,000 tons of supplies in 24 hours. West Berlin had survived and stood up to the Soviet Union. However, for Stalin it was a defeat and a humiliation as he had not been able to prevent the airlift from supplying West Berlin and had been forced to back down and reopen road and rail routes.

Another consequence of the Berlin Crisis of 1948–49 was the creation, in 1949, of the North Atlantic Treaty Organization. This was because the Berlin Crisis had confirmed Truman's commitment to Western Europe and convinced him that Western European states, even joined together, were no match for the Soviet Union and needed the formal support of the USA. NATO was signed by the USA, Canada, Britain and nine other countries of Western Europe and, although a defensive alliance, its main purpose was to prevent Soviet expansion.

The question is focused on through referring to the first consequence.
A detailed explanation of this consequence is given.
Precise evidence is given in this explanation.
The question is focused on through referring to the second consequence.
A detailed explanation of the second consequence is given.
Precise evidence is given in this explanation.

 The better answer

Below is an exam-style consequence question with two answers. Which is the better answer? Give three reasons why.

Explain two consequences of the creation of the Soviet invasion of Afghanistan.

ANSWER 1

In 1979, the Soviet Union invaded Afghanistan. The Soviets wanted to keep their influence in Afghanistan. President Carter was furious and criticised the invasion. Afghan rebels opposed the invasion. The USA supported these rebels. One consequence was that the USA refused to attend the Moscow Olympics of 1980.

ANSWER 2

One consequence of the Soviet invasion of Afghanistan was the Carter Doctrine. President Carter was furious with the invasion and introduced this doctrine which stated that the USA would use military force if necessary to defend its national interests in the Persian Gulf region. It also promised US military aid to all the countries bordering Afghanistan. In subsequent years, the USA gave military support to the *mujahideen*, Afghan rebels who fought against the Soviet occupation.

Another consequence of the Soviet invasion of Afghanistan was to end the period of *détente* between the superpowers. One feature of *détente* was the SALT talks. SALT 2 talks had begun in 1974 but, in 1969, the US Senate refused to ratify this agreement. *Détente* gave way to increased rivalry between the USA and the Soviet Union and the beginning of the Second Cold War. In retaliation to the Soviet invasion, the USA boycotted the Moscow Olympics of 1980.

1 _____

2 _____

3 _____

Question 2: Narrative account

Below is an example of an exam-style narrative question which is worth 8 marks.

Write a narrative account analysing the ways in which relations between the USA and the Soviet Union worsened in the years 1979–85.

> You may use the following information in your answer:
> - Soviet invasion of Afghanistan (1979)
> - Strategic Defence Initiative
>
> You **must** also use information of your own.

How to answer

- Look for the key points in the question and <u>underline them</u>.
- You can choose to write about the two events given in the question and an event of your own, or write entirely about events of your own.
- If you write about the events in the question make sure you write about at least three events. Including three events is important because you *must bring in an event of your own*.
- Ensure that your events are in the correct chronological sequence.
- Ensure that you give detail about each of the events you write about.
- Use linking words between each event and the next. Try to use phrases such as 'this led to', 'as a result of this'.

Below is a sample answer to this exam-style narrative question with comments around it.

In 1979, relations between the USA and the Soviet Union worsened because of the Soviet invasion of Afghanistan. Between 25 December 1979 and 1 January 1980, more than 50,000 Soviet troops were sent to Afghanistan to restore order and protect the People's Democratic Party of Afghanistan (PDPA) from the Muslim guerrilla movement known as the *mujahideen*. The US president was furious with the Soviet Union and took a tough line. He introduced the Carter Doctrine stated that the USA would use military force if necessary to defend its national interests in the Persian Gulf region. It also promised US military aid to all the countries bordering Afghanistan.

> Using the words of the question gives immediate focus.

> There is a developed analysis of the first event, using precise details.

As a result of Carter's get tough policy, relations continued to worsen and there was a Second Cold War. The Senate delayed passing the SALT 2 treaty and the USA cancelled all shipments of grain to the Soviet Union and US companies were forbidden to sell high-technology equipment there, such as computers and oil-drilling tools. Moreover, Carter pressured the US Olympic Committee to boycott the Moscow Olympic Games of 1980. Sixty-one other countries followed Carter's example. Superpower politics had now intruded into the Olympics. Indeed, the Soviet Union retaliated by boycotting the Los Angeles Olympics of 1984.

> A link is made between the first and second events. An event not given in the question is introduced.

> There is a developed analysis of the second event.

Superpower relations during this Second Cold War were further worsened by Reagan and the Strategic Defence Initiative. Reagan believed in taking a far tougher line with the Soviet Union than Carter. He made it clear that he had no interest in *détente* and was prepared to confront the Soviet Union whenever possible. Reagan's plan was to launch an army of satellites equipped with powerful lasers, which would intercept Soviet missiles in space and destroy them before they could do any harm to the USA. The Soviet Union was furious. Soviet leaders knew that they could not compete with Reagan's 'Star Wars' plan. They were behind the USA in space and computer technology whilst the Soviet economy was not producing enough wealth to fund even more defence spending.

> A link is made between the second and third events.

> There is a developed analysis of the third event.

'Through the eyes' of the examiner

Below is an exam-style narrative question with part of a sample answer. It would be useful to look at this answer 'through the eyes' of an examiner. The examiner will look for the following:

- events in the correct sequence
- clear links between events
- an explanation of each event.

You need to:

- highlight words or phrases which show that the answer has focused on the question
- underline where attempts are made to show links between one event and the next
- in the margin, write a word or phrase which sums up each specific explanation as it appears.

Write a narrative account analysing the main events in rivalry between the USA and the Soviet Union in the years 1948–56.

> **You may use the following information in your answer:**
> - Berlin Crisis (1948–49)
> - Warsaw Pact (1955)
>
> You **must** also use information of your own.

The first event which increased rivalry between the superpowers was the Berlin Crisis of 1948–49. On 24 June 1948, Stalin accused the West of interfering in the Soviet zone. He cut off road, rail and canal traffic in the attempt to starve West Berlin. Truman was determined to stand up to the Soviet Union and show that he was serious about containment. The only way into Berlin was by air. So the Allies decided to airlift supplies from their bases in West Germany. The airlift began on 28 June 1948 and lasted for ten months and was the start of the biggest airlift in history. The airlift continued into the spring and reached its peak on 16–17 April 1949 when 1398 flights landed nearly 13,000 tons of supplies in 24 hours. In May 1949, Stalin lifted the blockade. It greatly increased East–West rivalry. Truman saw the crisis as a great victory. West Berlin had survived and stood up to the Soviet Union. For Stalin it was a defeat and a humiliation. It led to the creation of the North Atlantic Treaty Organisation or NATO, which Stalin saw as an alliance aimed against the Soviet Union.

In retaliation to the establishment of NATO, in 1955 the Soviet Union set up the Warsaw Pact, which further increased rivalry between the two superpowers. It was a military alliance of eight nations headed by the Soviet Union and was designed to counter the threat of NATO. Members were to support each other if attacked. A joint command structure was set up under the Soviet Supreme Commander. This meant that there were now two major alliance systems – NATO and the Warsaw Pact – with each determined to be stronger than the other, which, in turn, intensified the arms race with the development of even more powerful weapons of mass destruction.

 Adding a third event

The answer above does not include a third event. What would you choose as a third event and why? Try completing the answer, remembering to add details to support your chosen event.

Question 3: Importance

Below is an exam-style question.

Explain two of the following:

- The importance of the Hungarian uprising (1956) for the development of the Cold War.
- The importance of the Cuban Missile Crisis (1962) for relations between the USA and the Soviet Union.
- The importance of the Soviet invasion of Czechoslovakia (1968) for the development of the Cold War.

How to answer

- You must choose **two** of these three developments. Your choice should be based on the two you feel provide greater opportunity for you to focus on *importance*.

- For the two you have chosen <u>underline key points</u> in the question. This will ensure that you focus sharply on what the question wants you to write about.

- Remember for each development that you choose that the focus of the question is its *importance* for a further factor and/or event.

Below is a part of a sample answer to this exam-style importance question with comments around it.

The Hungarian uprising was important for the development of the Cold War because it demonstrated Soviet determination to maintain control in Eastern Europe and worsened relations between the two superpowers. In October 1956, demonstrations against Soviet control began, Khrushchev sent troops and tanks to Budapest to try to restore peace and, on 26 October, Nagy was reinstated as prime minister. Nagy held talks with the Soviet Union and it was agreed that the tanks would be withdrawn. On 31 October, Nagy's proposed reforms were published. His most controversial decision was his intention to withdraw Hungary from the Warsaw Pact. On 4 November, Khrushchev decided that Nagy had gone too far, and 200,000 Soviet troops and 6000 tanks returned to Hungary. Khrushchev was able to keep control, and a new Soviet-backed leader, Kádár, was installed. Nagy was arrested and shot in 1958.

> There is an immediate focus on the key word of the question: importance.

> A developed explanation is given using precise details.

There was very little that the West, especially the USA and Britain, could do, apart from condemn the actions of the Soviet Union, to help the Hungarians. Hungary was too far away for military intervention. Britain, France and the USA were preoccupied with the Suez Crisis. The crisis was important because it highlighted the determination of the Soviet Union to maintain its control of Eastern Europe and prevent any further attacks on Communist control. It was also important because it intensified superpower rivalry. The USA was furious with the brutal suppression of the uprising by the Soviet Union. American criticism infuriated the Soviet Union who regarded Eastern Europe as their sphere of influence.

> The importance of the Hungarian uprising is focused on again.

Below is the second part of the answer to the exam-style importance question and a mark scheme.

1   Read the answer and the mark scheme. Decide which level you would award the paragraph. Write the level below, along with a justification for your choice.

Mark scheme		
Level	**Mark**	
1	1–2	A simple or generalised answer is given, showing limited development, organisation of material and limited knowledge and understanding
2	3–5	An explanation is given is given showing some attempt to analyse importance. It shows some reasoning, but may lack organisation. Accurate and relevant information is added
3	6–8	An explanation is given, showing analysis of importance, and is well structured. Accurate and relevant knowledge is included. It shows good knowledge and understanding of the required characteristics of the period

The Soviet invasion of Czechoslovakia increased East–West rivalry during the Cold War. The 'Prague Spring' refers to a series of reforms introduced by Dubček. The reforms included greater political freedom including free speech and the abolition of press censorship. Soon after, hundreds and thousands of Soviet troops entered Czechoslovakia. Czechs threw petrol bombs at the Soviet tanks as they moved through Prague. Buildings were set on fire and protesters assembled in Wenceslas Square. The Soviet invasion gave rise to the Brezhnev Doctrine which said that all member countries had to remain part of the Warsaw Pact. Britain and the USA protested at Soviet actions. The USA did nothing else because they were fighting in Vietnam. The Soviet invasion was important because it worsened relations.

Level [   ]   Reason _____
_____

2   Now suggest what the student has to do to achieve a higher level.

_____
_____
_____
_____

3   Try and rewrite this part of the answer at a higher level.

4   Now try and write an answer for the second bullet in the exam-style importance question.

Revision techniques

We all learn in different ways and if you're going to be successful in your revision you need to work out the ways that work best for you. Remember that revision doesn't have to be dull and last for hours at a time – but it is really important you do it! The highest grades are awarded to students who have consistently excellent subject knowledge and this only comes with solid revision.

Method 1: 'Brain dumps'

These are particularly useful when done every so often – it's never too early to start! Take a big piece of paper or even a whiteboard and write down everything you can remember about the topic you are revising, one of the units or even the whole History course. You could write down:

- dates
- names of key individuals
- key events
- important place names
- anything else you can remember.

Once you're satisfied you can't remember any more, use different colours to highlight or underline the words in groups. For example, when revising the Cuban Missile Crisis you might choose to underline all the mentions that relate to the causes in red and to the effects in blue.

You could extend this task by comparing your brain dump with that of a friend. The next time you do it, try setting yourself a shorter time limit and see if you can write down more.

Method 2: Learning walks

Make use of your space! Write down key facts and place them around your home, where you will see them every day. Make an effort to read the facts whenever you walk past them. You might decide to put information on the early Cold War on the stairs with the idea of the Cold War steadily developing.

Method 3: 'Distilling'

Memory studies show that we retain information better if we revisit it regularly. This means that revising the information once is not necessarily going to help it stay in your brain. Going back over the facts at intervals of less than a week leads to the highest retention of facts.

To make this process streamlined, try 'distilling' your notes. Start by reading over the notes you've completed in class or in this revision guide; two days later, read over them again, and this time write down everything you didn't remember. If you repeat this process enough you will end up with hardly any facts left to write down, because they will all be stored in your brain, ready for the exam!

Method 4: Using your downtime

There are always little pockets of time through the day which aren't much good for anything: bus journeys, queues, ad breaks in TV programmes, waiting for the bath to run and so on. If you added all these minutes up it would probably amount to quite a lot of time, which can be put to good use for revision.

Instead of having to carry around your notes, though, make use of something you carry around with you already. Most of us have a phone that can take pictures and record voice memos, or an iPod or something similar:

- Photograph key sections of this book and read over them.
- Record yourself reading information so that you can listen back over it – while you're playing football, before you go to sleep, or any other time.

Access the quizzes that go with this book at www.hoddereducation.co.uk/myrevisionnotes

Answers

Page 5: Organising knowledge

	Tehran	Yalta	Potsdam
Points agreed	Britain and the USA agreed to open up a second front by invading France in May 1944 The Soviet Union was to wage war against Japan once Germany was defeated A United Nations Organisation was to be set up after the war An area of eastern Poland was added to the Soviet Union	The Soviet Union would enter the war against Japan once Germany had surrendered To divide Germany and Berlin into four zones: US, British, French and Soviet To hunt down and try Nazi war criminals in an international court of justice To allow countries that had been liberated from occupation by the German army to have free elections Setting up a United Nations Organisation	To divide Germany and Berlin as previously agreed Germany had to pay reparations to the Allies in equipment and materials De-Nazification. To ban the Nazi Party. Nazis were removed from important positions and leading Nazis were put on trial for war crimes at Nuremberg in 1946 That Poland's frontier was to be moved westwards to the rivers Oder and Neisse Full participation in UN
Areas of disagreement		On how much Germany was to pay in reparations. Stalin wanted a much higher figure than either Roosevelt or Churchill About Poland – Stalin wanted a 'friendly' Polish government	Over what to do about Germany. Stalin wanted massive compensation but Truman refused Truman wanted free elections in the countries of Eastern Europe occupied by Soviet troops. Stalin did not The atomic bomb. Stalin was convinced that the USA was using the bomb as a warning to the Soviet Union
Importance in causing tensions	First meeting of three Allied leaders	Settled fate of Germany after the war Last meeting of three leaders as Roosevelt died soon after	Last of these Allied meetings Highlighted differences between East and West over Poland and Germany
Consequences	Led to disagreements over Poland	Led to disagreements over German reparations and Soviet actions in Poland	Led to major differences over different zones in Germany and ultimately Berlin Crisis

Page 7: Eliminate irrelevance

The Soviet Union took control of the countries in Eastern Europe by rigging to ensure that Soviet-controlled Communist parties took over. These countries included Bulgaria, Romania, Hungary, Poland and Czechoslovakia.

One of the consequences of the creation of these states was security for the Soviet Union. The Soviet Union had been invaded from the west by Germany on two occasions, in 1914 and 1941, and had suffered huge casualties during the ensuing world wars. Stalin created Soviet-controlled states in Eastern Europe as a buffer against future invasions.

The 'Novikov telegram' was written by Nikolai Novikov, who was the Soviet ambassador to the USA at the time. He accused the USA of trying to achieve world dominance. Another consequence was increased rivalry. The USA, Britain and France believed that Stalin's motives were political – the expansion of the Soviet empire and communism throughout Europe.

Explain **two** consequences of the Potsdam Conference:

- Led to differences over Germany. Stalin wanted massive compensation but Truman refused. He saw a revived Germany as a possible barrier to future Soviet expansion.
- Increased rivalry between East and West because of the atomic bomb. Stalin was convinced that the USA was using the bomb as a warning to the Soviet Union.

Page 9: RAG: Rate the timeline

- ★ **1941** The formation of the Grand Alliance
- ★ **1943** The Tehran Conference
- ★ **1945** The Yalta Conference
- ★ **1945** The USA exploded the first atomic bombs
- ★ **1945** Potsdam Conference
- ★ **1946** Long and Novikov telegrams
- ★ **1947** Truman Doctrine and Marshall Plan
- ★ **1947** The setting up of Cominform
- ★ **1948** Beginning of Berlin blockade
- ★ **1949** The setting up of NATO
- ★ **1955** The setting up of the Warsaw Pact
- ★ **1956** The Hungarian uprising

Page 11: Develop the detail

The Potsdam Conference was important because it led to differences between the Soviet Union and the USA over Germany. Stalin wanted massive compensation but Truman refused. He saw a revived Germany as a possible barrier to future Soviet expansion. It also led to differences between the two superpowers over what should happen to countries in Eastern Europe. Truman wanted free elections in the countries of Eastern Europe occupied by Soviet troops. Stalin did not.

Page 11: Spot the mistakes

The Truman Doctrine of 1946 was important because it led to American support for the Greek government, which was now able to defeat communism. The USA became committed to a policy of containment and became far more involved in the affairs of Europe. It was also important because it led to the Marshall Plan, which provided economic aid to Europe.

Page 13: Consequences and importance

Event	Consequences	Importance
The Truman Doctrine	US support for Greece, which was able to defeat threat from communism It led to the setting up of the Marshall Plan	Worsened relations due to US policy of containment
The Marshall Plan	Led to US economic aid for countries in Western Europe Soviet Union set up Comecon	Further divided East and West as Soviet Union not allow satellite states to get aid
Berlin Crisis	Confirmed that West would remain in West Berlin Led to setting up of NATO	First major crisis and greatly increased rivalry between superpowers
NATO	Committed USA to the defence of Europe Led to rival alliance – the Warsaw Pact	Further intensified rivalry – Stalin convinced that NATO was aimed against Soviet Union
Arms race	Led to build-up of ever more destructive weapons – atomic bomb followed by hydrogen bomb	Increased rivalry as each side spent more and more on weapons
Warsaw Pact	Strengthened military position of Soviet Union	Now had two rival alliance systems – intensified rivalry and arms race

Page 13: Matching dates and events

D Potsdam Conference
G Long telegram
A Truman Doctrine
F Beginning of the blockade of Berlin

C Setting up of NATO
E Soviet Union tested the H-bomb
B Setting up of the Warsaw Pact

Page 15: You're the examiner

Low level 2. A narrative is given showing some organisation of material into a sequence of events leading to an outcome. Accurate and relevant knowledge is added, showing some knowledge and understanding of the events. Only focuses on the two stimulus points.

Student needs to analyse the linkage between the events and include events prompted by the stimulus points.

Page 17: Identifying consequences

Statement	Cause	Event	Consequence
The flow of refugees was stopped. It led to the Cuban Missile Crisis of 1962			✓
On 13 August 1961, Khrushchev closed the border between East and West Berlin		✓	
The construction of the Berlin Wall led to a serious stand-off between the two superpowers			✓
Between 1949 and 1961, about 4 million East Germans fled to the West through Berlin	✓		
The East German officials replaced the makeshift wall with one that was sturdier and more difficult to scale		✓	
It led to the Cuban Missile Crisis of 1962			✓
East German troops and workers installed barbed-wire entanglements and fences		✓	
The Soviet Union claimed that the USA and its Allies used West Berlin as a base for espionage	✓		

Page 17: How important

Factor	Very important	Important	Quite important
Berlin Wall	It led to a stand-off between the two superpowers		
The Paris Summit, 1960		Khrushchev stormed out of conference, which meant no solution to the Berlin problem	
Kennedy's visit to Berlin			Showed US commitment to West Berlin and infuriated Soviet Union and Khrushchev

Page 19: You're the examiner

Level 2   Mark 4

Reason: Narrative which shows some organisation but limited linkage. Only explains two factors.

Now suggest what the student has to do with this paragraph to achieve the next level:

- needs to show how the events led to the outcome
- demonstrate linkage between the events
- explain a third factor.

Page 21: Relevance

Statements	R	PR	I
The Soviet invasion temporarily worsened relations between East and West	R		
In the 1960s, there was growing opposition to Soviet control of Czechoslovakia			I
Western European countries condemned the invasion but provided no military help	R		
Some Communists, including Ceausescu of Romania, began to move away from Moscow	R		
On 20–21 August 1968, hundreds and thousands of Warsaw Pact troops entered Czechoslovakia		PR	
Czechs threw petrol bombs at the Soviet tanks as they moved through Prague		PR	
Novotný had been the Czech leader since 1957 and was unpopular because he was a hardline Communist			I
It gave rise to the Brezhnev Doctrine. This redefined communism as a one-party state	R		
Many Czechs began to demand greater democracy, including Dubček			I
During the Soviet invasion, buildings were set on fire and protesters assembled in Wenceslas Square		PR	
The 'Prague Spring' refers to a series of reforms introduced by Dubček in the spring of 1968		PR	
In January 1969, Jan Palach, a student, set fire to himself in Wenceslas Square to protest against the Soviet invasion	R		

Quick quizzes at **www.hoddereducation.co.uk/myrevisionnotes**

Page 23: Organising knowledge

Meaning of *détente*	This was attempts to improve relations and relax tension between the USA and Soviet Union in the 1970s as both sides wished to reduce their spending on the arms race
SALT 1	The two superpowers agreed that there would be no further production of strategic ballistic missiles
	It was significant because it was the first agreement between the superpowers that successfully limited the number of nuclear weapons they held
Helsinki Agreements	These were signed in 1975 between the USA and the Soviet Union, along with 33 other nations
	They signed agreements known as baskets about security, cooperation and human rights
	This was the high point of *détente*
SALT 2	SALT 2 began in 1974 and the treaty was signed in June 1979
	The two superpowers agreed on further arms limitations
	However, the US Senate refused to ratify the SALT 2 agreements following the Soviet invasion of Afghanistan, December 1979

Page 23: Linking events

The Strategic Arms Limitation Talks began in 1969 and were completed three years later. The two superpowers agreed that there would be no further production of strategic ballistic missiles and that submarines carrying nuclear weapons would only be introduced when existing stocks of intercontinental ballistic missiles became obsolete.

As a result of SALT 1, there were improved relations between the superpowers which led to the Helsinki Agreements which were signed in 1975. The USA and the USSR, along with 33 other nations, made declarations about three distinct international issues. Each signatory at Helsinki agreed to respect human rights and basic freedoms such as thought, speech, religion and freedom from unfair arrest. Also at Helsinki there was a recognition of Europe's frontiers. The Soviet Union accepted the existence of West Germany.

The improved relations at Helsinki were also shown in 1975 by a joint space mission in which an American Apollo spacecraft and a Soviet Soyuz spacecraft docked high above Earth. This marked the beginning of superpower cooperation in space. This seemed to be further confirmed by SALT 2 which was signed in June 1979. However, the US Senate refused to ratify the SALT 2 agreements following the Soviet invasion of Afghanistan, December 1979.

Page 27: RAG: Rate the timeline

- ★ **1972** SALT 1 signed
- ★ **1974** Nixon visited Moscow
- ★ **1975** The Helsinki Agreements
- ★ **1979** SALT 2 signed
- ★ **1979** Soviet invasion of Afghanistan
- ★ **1979** Carter Doctrine
- ★ **1979** US Congress refused to ratify SALT 2
- ★ **1980** USA boycotted Moscow Olympics
- ★ **1981** Reagan became US president and described the Soviet Union as the 'evil empire'
- ★ **1983** Reagan announced the Strategic Defence Initiative

- ★ **1984** USSR boycotted Los Angeles Olympics
- ★ **1985** Reagan and Gorbachev met for the first time at the Geneva summit
- ★ **1986** Reykjavík summit
- ★ **1987** Intermediate Nuclear Forces Treaty
- ★ **1989** Pulling down of the Berlin Wall
- ★ **1990** Collapse of the Soviet Union
- ★ **1990** Baltic states of Estonia, Latvia and Lithuania declared themselves independent
- ★ **1990** START
- ★ **1991** Gorbachev resigned
- ★ **1991** Warsaw Pact was formally ended

Page 27: Develop the detail

The invasion of Afghanistan was important because it ended the period of *détente* and increased rivalry between the Soviet Union and the USA. The USA was furious with the Soviet invasion which threatened US interests in the area. It was important because it led to the Carter Doctrine. The Carter Doctrine stated that the USA would use military force if necessary to defend its national interests, especially oil interests, in the Persian Gulf region. It also promised US military aid to all the countries bordering Afghanistan. It was also important because it led to the USA boycotting the Moscow Olympics of 1980. Sixty-one other countries followed Carter's example. The Soviet Union retaliated four years later by boycotting the Los Angeles Olympic Games.

Page 29: Organising knowledge

State	Developments	Importance
Poland	In 1988 there were strikes throughout the country. In the following year Solidarity won elections	Mazowiecki became the first non-communist Prime Minister in Eastern Europe
Czechoslovakia	In November 1989, huge demonstrations against communism led to the resignation of the Communist government. This was known as the 'Velvet Revolution'	Havel became the first non-Communist Czech president since 1948
East Germany	In October 1989, Gorbachev visited East Germany and said that Soviet troops would not put down East German demonstrations. These demonstrations led to the pulling down of the Berlin Wall in November 1989	Main symbol of the Cold War now destroyed and free movement between East and West Berlin for first time since 1961
Romania	In 1989, huge demonstrations against President Ceausescu who fled but was later captured in 1990 Democratic elections won by National Salvation Front containing many non-Communists	The downfall of one of the most hated Communist dictators and the setting up of a new government including non-Communists
Bulgaria	In 1990, Democratic elections won by renamed Communist Party	First democratic government since late 1940s
Hungary	In 1988, Gorbachev accepted that Hungary could become a multi-party state. In the following year the Democratic elections were won by Democratic Forum, an alliance of non-Communist groups. In October 1989, the opening of Hungary's borders to East Germans and the West	Events in Hungary encouraged developments in East Germany and especially the pulling down of the Berlin Wall

Page 31: Complete the paragraph

> One consequence of the collapse of the Soviet Union was the ending of the Cold War. As Soviet control of Eastern Europe fell away, it became obvious that the Warsaw Pact could not survive. The pact was an alliance that united the Communist states of Eastern Europe against the capitalist states of the West. This marked the end of the Cold War.
>
> A second consequence was the break-up of the Soviet Union. The many nationalities and ethnic groups saw how the satellite states had been able to break away from Moscow.
>
> In 1990, the Baltic states of Estonia, Latvia and Lithuania declared themselves independent, which was accepted by Moscow in 1991. This led to other demands for independence within the Soviet Union.

Page 31: How important

Factor	Key features	Decisive/Important/Quite important
Gorbachev's 'new thinking'	In 1988, Gorbachev rejected the Brezhnev Doctrine and in 1989 he accepted that members of the Warsaw Pact could make changes to their own countries without expecting outside interference. This became known as the Sinatra Doctrine	Decisive because it encouraged the growth of opposition to communism in Eastern Europe and the eventual overthrow of Communist governments
Summit conferences	Series of meetings between Gorbachev, Reagan and Bush in the years 1986–91 which discussed arms limitations	Important because led to agreements such as the INF and greatly reduced tension between the superpowers
Fall of the Berlin Wall	Demonstrations in East Germany led to the pulling down of the Berlin Wall in November 1989	Decisive because it removed the main symbol of East–West rivalry and the Iron Curtain
INF	It was the first treaty to reduce the number of nuclear missiles that the superpowers possessed. It therefore went much further than SALT 1, which simply limited the growth of Soviet and US stockpiles	Quite important because it showed the willingness of both superpowers to limit the arms race
Collapse of the Soviet Union	In 1990, the Baltic states of Estonia, Latvia and Lithuania declared themselves independent, which was accepted by Moscow in 1991. Gorbachev resigned in December 1991 and the Soviet Union split into several independent states. Now there was only one superpower left – the USA	Decisive as now there was only one superpower – the USA. The Warsaw Pact ended as a result of the collapse of the Soviet Union

Page 33: Question 1: Consequence

Give three reasons why the Level 2 answer is better than the Level 1 answer:

- The Level 2 answer is far more explicit in focusing on the question by using phrases such as 'The first consequence'.
- The Level 2 answer includes specific information about the consequence to support the explanation.
- The supporting information is precise and shows good knowledge and understanding of the period.

Page 35: 'Through the eyes' of the examiner

You need to:

- Underline where attempts are made to show links between one event and the next.
- In the margin write a word or phrase which sums up each specific explanation as it appears.
- Highlight words or phrases used which show that the answer has focused on the question.

The first event which increased rivalry between superpowers was the Berlin Crisis of 1948–49. On 24 June 1948, Stalin accused the West of interfering in the Soviet zone. He cut off road, rail and canal traffic in the attempt to starve West Berlin. Truman was determined to stand up to the Soviet Union and show that he was serious about containment. The only way into Berlin was by air. So the Allies decided to airlift supplies from their bases in West Germany. The airlift began on 28 June 1948 and lasted for ten months and was the start of the biggest airlift in history. The airlift continued into the spring and reached its peak on 16–17 April 1949 when 1398 flights landed nearly 13,000 tons of supplies in 24 hours. In May 1949, Stalin lifted the blockade. It greatly increased East–West rivalry. Truman saw the crisis as a great victory. West Berlin had survived and stood up to the Soviet Union. For Stalin it was a defeat and a humiliation. It led to the creation of the North Atlantic Treaty Organisation or NATO, which Stalin saw as an alliance aimed against the Soviet Union.

In retaliation to the establishment of NATO, in 1955 the Soviet Union set up the Warsaw Pact, which further increased rivalry between the two superpowers. It was a military alliance of eight nations headed by the Soviet Union and was designed to counter the threat of NATO. Members were to support each other if attacked. A joint command structure was set up under the Soviet Supreme Commander. This meant that there were now two major alliance systems – NATO and the Warsaw Pact – with each determined to be stronger than the other, which, in turn, intensified the arms race with the development of even more powerful weapons of mass destruction.

Possible third points:

- NATO 1949
- arms race
- Hungarian uprising 1956.

Page 36: You're the examiner

This is a level 3 answer, 8 marks:

- strong focus on importance
- the importance is supported by a strong explanation which includes relevant and precise information.

Improving the answer:

- First improvement. Ensure relevant to the question. The Prague Spring is not directly relevant to the question.
- Second improvement. More explicit focus on importance.